A Walk Through Asia

Sandy Solomon

A Walk Through Asia

By Sandy Solmon

ImPress Publishing Services
Orlando, Florida
NewhouseCreativeGroup.com
2025, Sandy Solomon

Names: Solomon, Sandy
Title: A Walk Through Asia / by Sandy Solomon
Description: Orlando, FL | ImPress Publishing Services. | Summary: I experienced being a part of a culture different from the norm of where I live.
ISBN 978-1-945493-85-0 (paperback)

Dedicated to my family and sharing our lives.

Chapter 1

Prelude

Working as a Travel Agent gave me an opportunity to travel the world... And what an adventure it was!

I was fortunate to win trips to different countries. My favorite destinations were in Asia as I welcomed the different cultures vs. Western civilizations.

$1000.00 award winner

I traveled with my husband, and except for China, which we viewed on a tour, and Indonesia, which we experienced from a cruise ship, we went to each country independently. Many times we hired a local guide to show us a particular region. It was an excellent way to get an in depth glimpse into the communities, and the lives they were living, or mores. The distances to reach our destinations were far, sometimes 12 hours. My husband would jokingly say, "are we there yet?". It just took some patience, and worth it.

The customs and traditions of Asia are as diverse and colorful as the continent itself. It offers that window into the rich tapestry of cultures that make up this vast and vibrant region. From festivals and tea ceremonies to martial arts and traditional clothing, these customs are not just practices, but a way of life that has been passed down through generations.

Asian cultural values generally emphasize family unity, respect for authority, and a strong work ethic. These values are often instilled from a young age, and play a significant role in shaping individual identities and behaviors.

Maintaining harmony with relationships and avoiding confrontation are important cultural scruples in many Asian societies. Humility and modesty are ideals, and individuals are often encouraged to downplay their accomplishments and avoid boasting.

In many Asian countries, respecting elders is a fundamental value that is deeply ingrained in society. From addressing elders with proper titles, to seeking their advise and guidance. The concept of honoring one's parents and ancestors is central, and is reflected in various customs and rituals. Many homes share their families, with elders living together with their children and grandchildren.

A strong emphasis is on formal education. In our school system in the United States, competitions among students mostly reveal Asian children at the top of the ladder. Asian Americans are winners year after year in the National Spelling Bees. The focus is also on math. They graduate with honors, and believe higher education goals to be of utmost importance.

As I traveled in the Asian countries, I was dismayed by their bathroom facilities. Particularly in Japan and China. They don't use commodes. When you need to use the toilet, there is a hole in the ground inside the stall. They believe it is more sanitary and healthy. In the Tokyo airport, selection can be made to use the Western or Eastern bathrooms. I wondered how the "geisha" girls handled using the toilet with all those garments. No problem in the hotels.

When I was in China, I had to gather toilet paper from a roll before I entered the stall. How do you know how much you'll need?

Has it changed over the years? Transitioning away from the use of toilet paper has been considered. It represents part of a broader shift toward more sustainable daily practices. Some companies now develop products incorporating water-activated cleansing agents. Some homes already use bidets. Who knows what the future will bring? That's a story for another time.

However, wherever we went in Asia, we were welcomed. People appeared pleased to see you, especially in 1988 when we began our visits. Not many non-Asians were visitors at that juncture. Surprisingly though, English was understood and spoken, probably because the British had been in those locales for many years earlier. My husband, Paul, was tall at 6'2" and towered over Asians who were of shorter stature.

We gathered replicas of each country, and placed them in our curio cabincts, to remind us always of our visits.

CHAPTER 2

HONG KONG

Our first Asian adventure was to Hong Kong in 1988. At the time we were there, it was before Britain gave it back to China in 1997.

In July 1898, after the Opium War, Hong Kong was ceded and leased to Britain for 100 years. In 1997, the British returned Hong Kong to China, with the agreement that it would maintain its Capitalist economy and retain a large degree of political autonomy for a period of 50 years, until 2047. The concept would be "One Country, Two Systems".

A controversial security law passed in 2020, however, that had the ability to weaken "One Country, Two Systems", and threatened the political autonomy as well as reduced civil liberties that the region had enjoyed. So the agreement was ignored. China has taken over Hong Kong, and as the rest of the population in China, they are under autocratic rule. Their independence is gone.

There were residents in the previous time, before the takeover, from many different countries, but those individuals have left.

On our visit in 1988, there were many modern skyscrapers on the smallest piece of real estate. Just flying into the airport is a feat to behold, as the plane lands among those buildings. The airport after 1988 is now a new larger facility, a distance away on one of the surrounding islands. About half of the population live on adjacent islands.

When it was an International city, it was a city of contrasts. There were so many distinctions between the residents from all over the world. We experienced eating in a Jewish deli for lunch, to having a delicious dinner on a Chinese floating boat. There was a maze of shops selling their wares from different countries, as we wandered about.

I purchased an unusual piece of luggage, that I was able to use for the rest of my trip. As I was going from country to country and making purchases or no longer needing a particular item, I placed it in the compartments. You didn't open that compartment until you arrived home.

It had 3 compartments that started out in a flat position. You filled the first compartment and then zippered it closed. On top of that, fill next compartment and zipper it closed, and as the luggage kept getting taller, you filled the last compartment and zippered it closed. If you're purchasing souvenirs, what a great way to travel.

There were major financial centers, and still are, of the Asia Pacific region, despite the fact it is without the services of a central bank. Though many multinational companies have shifted their regional headquarters, or reduced their Hong Kong presence, it remains a major financial hub.

Once a regional media hub, Hong Kong has seen closure of independent news; journalists and activists arrested; and decline in press freedom rankings globally.

School curriculum's have been revised to emphasize patriotism and Chinese identity. Many Hong Kongers have emigrated to the United Kingdom, Canada and Australia. The UK in 2021, created a pathway for eligible Hong Kong residents.

It is a unique place, none the less. A growing local identity has emerged, especially among the younger generations.

If we look beyond the political landscape, Hong Kong is a fascinating city that does blend East and West. It is still a mixed culture. Not only does the territory celebrate festivals and holidays of the East and the West, they enjoy Chinese New Year, Christmas and the Western New Year, besides multiple theater and arts. Motion pictures are produced every year, many of which attain International fame. Disneyland opened in 2005 on a nearby island.

Victoria Park shows stunning panoramic views of Hong Kong island and Victoria Harbor. There is Symphony Of Lights, which is a dazzling nightly light and sound show involving 40 plus buildings.

British colonial architecture stands beside modern skyscrapers and traditional Chinese buildings. It is also home to one the world's tallest buildings, the 118th story International Commerce Center.

We can see that Hong Kong is still a unique city with World Class urban experiences, cultural depth and natural beauty. While it retains much of its vibrancy, the post 1997 era has brought significant changes.

Its transformation, the contrasts between its colonial past, its capitalist energy and its evolving status within China, make it a deeply compelling place.

Chapter 3

Singapore

Welcome to Singapore. We came into Changi airport in 1988. The airport first opened in 1981, and when Singapore Airlines was born. We flew on Singapore Airlines, and the stewardesses looked so beautiful in their colorful ethnic outfits. Up until 2023, it has been rated the world's best airline.

Tallest hotel in the world

A private guide met us, introduced us to Singapore, and transferred us to the Westin Stamford Hotel. At that time, it was the tallest hotel in the world, at 73 stories high. Entertainment and a restaurant were on the roof enclosure, as we looked out on this beautiful city that we were going to explore.

It is a small island country and city-state, comprised of one main island and 63 satellite islands, just north of the equator. It had been part of Malaysia, just to the north, but in 1965, split, and became an independent republic. Actually, going back further in 1819, it was a trading post of the British empire, when the Stamford Raffles hotel opened. That hotel became famous with its Singapore Sling, a pink drink including gin, cherry brandy and lime juice that was created in 1915, making this the 110th anniversary of this cocktail. I seem to remember Humphrey Bogart in a movie sitting in Raffles with its famous drink.

Sadly, for Sandy and Paul, we never got to Raffles to taste this famous drink.

It is a highly developed country with its People's Action Party in charge. It has won its 14th successive election to extend its broken 6 decade rule since Singapore's 1965 independence, and from 1959 when they were in power just before.

It's a major aviation, financial and maritime shipping hub. Cruise ships are known to depart from its shores, which we actually experienced, when we took a cruise many years later. It ranks high in education, health care, quality of life, personal safety, infrastructure and housing.

Singapore's streets are extremely safe, with crime rates very low. We wandered on our own, even at night, with no fears. As a small country, it is focused on purpose. As they lost most of a generation to the use of drugs, the death penalty takes a role, believing that their residents will never again be compromised and die, from anyone selling drugs.

The multicultural population is around 6 million, and in recognition of the cultural identities of the major ethnic groups within the nation, Singapore has 4 official languages: English, Malay, Mandarin and Tamil. English is the common language with exclusive use in numerous public services. Multi-racialism is enshrined in the constitution and continues to shape national policies. Most of the residents are Chinese at 75% and followed by 13% Malay and 9% Indian. However, though English is the main spoken language, residents are mostly bilingual. Their mother-tongue as a second language is taught in their schools in order to preserve each individual's ethnic identity. We're all different. That's what makes us special. We have to love one another and recognize our differences. That's what they focus on in Singapore.

We took a "Contrasting Cultures" tour, which focused on the mix of Indian, Malay and Chinese cultures. Different from each other, but blending well. They took us to Indian, Malay and Chinese centers. It was delightful and awakening to learn about each group, and how they respect their diversity.

Singapore's health system ranks as the 6th overall in the world. They've had the longest life expectancy of any one country, with 84.8 years. Women can expect to live an average of 87.6 years with a smaller difference for men.

Tourism is more than double the population. There are many attractions to visit, arts and shopping. The Singapore Botanic Gardens is a UNESCO World Heritage site. It has 18 man-made trees, each loaded with intricate vertical gardens on the top. The colossal solar-powered super trees are part of the 250 acre Gardens By The Bay. The evening light show gives you a neon appreciation for Singapore's unique relationship with nature.

Other attractions include River Wonders which has 300 species of animals, and the Night Safari, when you can see 1500 animals cavorting in their natural habitat.

There are performing arts centers, flagship museums and touring exhibitions of arts and sciences. Literature is highly regarded and written in the 4 official languages. You realize why tourism is so compelling. Sports and recreation are very popular, and they've had winners in the Olympics.

“More uncles than you know you had”. Regardless of their age, Singapore's taxi drivers are typically called “uncle”. Jump into a cab and if you're lucky to be driven by a chatty taxi uncle, be prepared for a discussion from anything in International business to what's for dinner. And taxis are cheap, probably costing no more than $20.00. Singapore is compact and easy to get around, even using the trains, or just walking.

We walked into a store displaying art. There was an active wall hanging...flowing water...singing monkeys...talking creations between the trees.

Never saw a creation like that before. “Did we want to bring it home?...yes”, but couldn't.

Singapore also has a diverse music culture. Their variation of cuisine is touted as another reason to visit the country.

Being of the Jewish faith, we located a synagogue, and met with the Rabbi. As it was during the holiday of Passover, he gave us matzo, a component of the holiday, to take back to our hotel.

There appears to be no prejudices among the residents. I wish it was the same elsewhere.

For a small country, a city-state, they seem to have it all. I have a friend, whose 2 children, a daughter and a son, each live there, and believe it's the best.

CHAPTER 4

THAILAND

Thailand for many centuries was a monarchy under the name of Siam. I always think of "The King And I" movie in 1956, with Yul Brynner as the King of Siam. No one else could have played that role more perfectly. His co-star Deborah Kerr was the American teacher for his many, many children, and ended up teaching the King himself by showing him how to dance.

In 1932, the Absolute Monarchy ended, and became a Constitutional Monarchy. The name changed to Thailand in 1939, which means "Land Of The Free".

The country has since gone through the invasion of the Japanese; becoming a Communist society; military coups; years of Democracy; Fascism; and a return to Democracy, but with a King as its Monarch and the head of state. There is a national assembly with a Prime Minister as head of government. Think of Great Britain using a similar system of government.

Buddhism remains central to Thai culture, and most homes have shrines to the Buddha. The Thai continue to engage in many practices that are grounded in the traditional culture. Even the most contemporary new business enterprises are opened only after the owners have consulted an astrologer for an auspicious date. Middle class city dwellers are more likely to consult spirit mediums than are rural people.

We were only in Bangkok for a few days, but took the scene all in. Our private guide showed us a beautiful official building whose front was made of precious stones, jade and mother of pearl. On either side were statues of Buddha guarding the entry. It was stunning to behold.

The silk industry is a major focus. Our guide took us to a home where the resident was using silk to produce different items. She showed us how she had the means to spin the silk, so that it became cloth. It was quite enlightening, and I purchased a beautiful cloth scarf. However, as we wandered around the city later, we found a store that was selling silk cloth. The proprietor suggested they could make me an outfit in one day, if I pick out my favorite cloth. As I agreed to do it, they measured me for a blouse and a skirt that matched, and I came back the next day to retrieve the garments which fit perfectly. The skirt wraps around the body. It was inexpensive and I loved it. I still have the skirt and wear it occasionally.

Floating market

When we were still with our guide, he brought us to a floating market, called Damnen Saduak. It's a canal, and heavily laden with barges carrying fresh produce, and other goods, that are useful for the residents. They go up and down the river, and just pass their products to their customers on the banks of the river. It was interesting to see, and very popular. We saw residents living along the river, washing their clothes in the water, a ritual that was part of their lives.

The Grand Palace in Bangkok was built in 1782. This ornate royal palace complex now houses a museum, and is open to visitors. The famous Wat Pho, known as the Temple Of The Reclining Buddha, is located nearby. There are many Buddhist Temples to see in Bangkok with depictions of Buddha.

We hired a tuk-tuk, which is a 3 wheeled motorcycle, to get around. He darted in and out of traffic, not staying in his lane. He commented that since Thailand means free land, you don't have to follow the rules. I kept my eyes closed through much of the trip. Didn't hop on a tuk-tuk again.

Eating in Thailand is quite an experience. Cuisine is a burst of spicy food, but it didn't work well with my palate. I kept pushing what I ordered towards my husband, who had no trouble with the spices. I recall when we returned home to Tampa, Florida after the trip, our friends were all excited about a Thai restaurant opening there. No way was I going! "Oh, you can ask for it milder", they said. Over the years I've gone to many Thai restaurants, asked for it mild, and enjoyed. Over time, I've begun to tolerate it more and don't even mention mild...or maybe they just don't spice it up like in Thailand.

At that time of year, in late March, it was very hot. We took an excursion to an area outside the city, and watched cultural performances that were very enjoyable. As it was so hot, wet iced washcloths were passed down the aisles to cool us off.

Thailand is known for its tropical beaches, opulent royal palaces and ancient ruins. Large Buddhas are present throughout the country. If you have time, get on a train and travel to other areas.

Ayuthaya is the capital of ancient Siam, and a UNESCO World Heritage site, with its ancient temples. A huge Buddha is on display.

Buddha

Khao Yai national park lies east of Ayuthaya and home to herds of wild elephants, as well as bears, rare birds, and barking deer. I remember hearing about people riding elephants in that region, but I'm sure those elephants were of a calmer nature. I recently read about wild elephants raiding homes and stores in search of food. This was happening as people continue to move into their environment near the national park. Try to picture these huge animals in their raids?

Another unusual area is Song Pong, a sleepy little district riddled with limestone formations that are home to more than 200 cave systems. You can glide through the most visited cave on a bamboo raft and look out for the ancient teak coffins that are perched there.

Back in Bangkok, Song Kran, the Thai New Year, takes place between the 13 and 15th day of April each year. In the Temples across the city, scented water is poured over people to symbolize the coming year. As the festival takes place during

Thailand's hottest month, it tends to culminate in less spiritual, family friendly public water fights in the streets. You certainly get to cool off. There are many ways to celebrate a New Year, but I thought getting water poured on you, was a blast!

In a short amount of time though, we were able to enjoy a very interesting destination.

Interlude...

My friends Jerry and Sunny were in Tokyo on a 3 year assignment for IBM. In the last year, 1988, they wrote and told us that before they leave Japan, come and visit us and we will be your guides. We took them up on their invitation, and planned the trip. As we didn't know if we'd ever get to Asia again, we decided to visit Hong Kong, Singapore and Thailand before arriving in Tokyo. And so here we are, as we followed through on that plan. It was the beginning of

April. Our friends told us the cherry blossoms will be in bloom when we arrive. (Cherry Blossoms are also in bloom in Washington, DC around that time. The forecast is arbitrary. Not an exact timing.)

We're flying out of Bangkok, leaving the hottest place on earth, or so we think. We land in Tokyo, step onto the tarmac, where there's snow on the ground. The cherry blossoms are in bloom, and as a backdrop, white snow.

Chapter 5

Japan

Our arrival in Tokyo was exciting as we were welcomed by our friends, Jerry and Sunny, who were in the latter part of a 3 year assignment from IBM. What an opportunity for them, as they lived in an apartment in the heart of Tokyo. It was paid for by IBM, who also covered the cost of paying the mortgage on their home in Tampa, Florida during their stay in Japan. We were living in Tampa. Our arrangement was to watch over their house, and make sure that everything was copacetic.

We are staying with them for a week, and they introduced us to Japan as our tour guides. Showing us around, we noted that prices compared to where we lived were exorbitant. Mainly produce, because some were imported. The price of a cantaloupe was around $25.00. So you purchased it for special occasions. We decided one evening to take them out for dinner, and asked for suggestions. They opted for Italian. So we're in Japan, eating in an Italian restaurant, and each of us ordered a pasta selection. The cost for the 4 of us was over $150.00.

The Japanese restaurants showed many of their selections from their menu in the store windows, so it was easier for us to make a choice. We enjoyed trying many different dishes throughout our stay.

We asked our hosts about their lives in Tokyo. Sunny was not allowed to work, not being a citizen, but there were many women from other countries that were there temporarily, and they shared their time together.

Jerry talked about his job working with the Japanese, and though he didn't know the language, managed quite well in his office representing IBM. He told us he had tried to learn the language, inviting an instructor into his home in the evenings, but said it was too difficult for him, so he gave up. Many of his co-workers spoke English, and it was evident throughout. When traveling in Japan, especially if you're in one of the big cities, you'll generally have no problem not speaking Japanese at all. There are usually English signs all over the train stations and local amusements.

Japan is a democracy, Unitary State, Parliamentary System, and Constitutional Monarchy. A Unitary State is a state governed as a single entity, in which the central government is the supreme authority. They still have an emperor.

The Imperial Palace sits among large public gardens. Tokyo, as Japan's busy capital mixes the ultramodern with traditional, from neon lit skyscrapers to historic temples.

There are Buddhist Temples and Shinto shrines. Shinto is focused on nature spirits and ancestors, emphasizing purity, harmony with nature and respect for ancestors. No founder or prophet is acknowledged.

Buddhism is a philosophy focusing on enlightenment and the path to end suffering through practices like meditation and compassion.

While they differ in core beliefs, they have also interacted with each other in Japan, based on teachings of Buddha. While many Japanese individuals identify with both Shinto and Buddhism, Shinto ceremonies are common for weddings, and Buddhist funerals are the norm.

My friends, Sunny and Jerry were invited to weddings because of their association with Jerry's co-workers. At the weddings, the attire for the ceremony was traditional where the bride wore an elegant kimono, and removed it for Western dress at the reception.

Kimono's have a major importance. There is a tradition for the intricate weaving technique that dates back more than a thousand years. Giant looms make patterns on the gorgeous fabric, slowly turning out from the loom that are repetitive and geometric. Deciding which hand-dyed color thread goes where to make the patterns is like the digital signals of a computer. You can understand why kimonos are in such demand.

Sunny started collecting kimonos. Just like the day after Thanksgiving here in the U.S., when people wake up early the next day to get a deal, Sunny did similarly. She waited for a very early event in Tokyo, when Kimonos were offered at a special price until it was sold out. When they returned to America, their 2 story homes had kimonos hanging off the balconies. They were quite beautiful.

Japanese culture places a high value on respect and courtesy. Bowing is a common form of greeting. We passed a phone booth, and looked at the local resident bowing during the conversation. It's just automatic.

Disney and Universal have their parks in residence. It seems, especially for Disney, they open in many countries. Ballparks are evident, because Japanese love baseball and major teams compete. Sumo wrestling is very popular. Jerry had his favorite wrestler who he followed religiously.

We went to a Kabuki opera. It is a major entertainment venue. Male actors play all the roles and become superstars. We were given an English synopsis of what we were watching so we could enjoy.

Theatrical Sensation!!
KABUKI SPECTACLE
SUPER KABUKI PIAY (3 Act)
Yamato Takeru
Matinee 11:00AM
Evening Show 4:30PM
SUPERSTAR ICHIKAWA ENNOSUKE
1988
Mar. 4th~Apr. 28th
UPERSTAR Ichikawa Ennosuke, versatile Kabuki actor
enjoys explosive popularity both at home and abroad,
mpersonate mythological hero Yamato Takeru who is
o have united Japan into a nation more about 2,000

As we traveled outside the city, we viewed beautiful architecture from past centuries. Our visit to Kyoto was outstanding. We took the bullet train, which is also quite an experience for its speed. It was hard to see the sites, as we were going so fast.

Kyoto is a separate island renowned as Japan's cultural capital due to its rich history; numerous temples and shrines; beautiful gardens and traditional culture. It was the capital of Japan in 794, and the Emperor's residence for over a thousand years until 1868, leading to the preservation of numerous historical and cultural landmarks. The Imperial Palace sits among large public gardens. At the onset of electricity, the Imperial Palace was the first place in Japan to have electric light. As one of the oldest cities, it's thought of as the heart of Japan. Palaces had geishas who were female entertainers, performing many types of roles, including sexual favors for the male elite.

At this juncture, I'd like to point out that Jerry told us that he was invited to a luncheon, when he was at work. It was a private room, and he wondered where the table was. He was told the table would be arriving. Out walks a nude woman who lies down across a wooden form, and becomes the table. The food is brought out on platters and lain on her body. The guests help themselves to the food, and touch the woman anywhere they desire. We couldn't believe what Jerry was telling us, but he gave us a magazine to verify it. It was called "A Day In The Life Of Japan", and there was the story that Jerry had related. Here we were in the 1980's, and women were still treated so vulnerable.

Back to Kyoto, we strolled around the squares, savoring the views. A few Japanese girls approached us, and were trying out their knowledge of English, giggling at their attempt. We enjoyed the moment.

In one area there were a large group of kid's sneakers lined up against the wall of a venue. We wondered how they would find their own shoes. On a building above the entrance were sculptures of monkeys depicting "Hear No Evil; Speak No Evil: See No Evil". Very familiar saying we should all adhere to.

Kyoto was spared from the bombing during World War II, including atomic attacks. It was largely due to the intervention of U.S. Secretary Of War, Henry Stimson, who argued that Kyoto's immense cultural and historic significance to Japan outweighed any military considerations. Nagasaki ultimately replaced Kyoto on the target list.

The U.S., did not drop an atomic bomb on Tokyo for several strategic reasons. Tokyo had already been heavily damaged by fire bombing. Secondly, Tokyo housed many government and military leaders, and a nuclear strike could have destabilized the Japanese command structure, potentially prolonging the war. Also, the Emperor was located there, and his death could have led to further resistance.

Other cities like Hiroshima and Nagasaki were chosen for their industrial importance and because they had been heavily damaged by previous bombing, allowing for a clearer demonstration of the bomb's power.

But as we look back to Japan as our enemy, they are now regarded as our ally, and welcomed reentry into our circle of other countries, with many agreements and connections. I'm glad they are now back with peace as their outlook.

The post-war Japanese miracle and the 1964 Summer Olympics allowed Tokyo to rebuild and grow. In 2018, Tokyo was the 2nd largest city in the world by population.

Consider the car industry. I've purchased Toyota's since the 1980's.

It's also a wonderful country to visit for its beauty and mostly peaceful history, architecture and its welcoming disposition.

INTERLUDE...

My daughter Debra, and son-in-law Mike, arranged for a Japanese exchange student, Keiko, to live with their family for a year. Keiko was 16 years old, and my granddaughter, Megan, who was 15, shared a room. In an adjacent room was my 13 year old grandson, Sean. Keiko could speak English, and took her Junior year at the same high school as Megan. They learned a lot from each other that year, and it was a wonderful experience for all. Keiko was a charming individual, and was treated like a member of the family. Living in Tampa at the time, we flew up to New York where this family resided, and visited with them as we met Keiko. Before the year was over, they all came to visit us in Tampa.

Once the year was over, Keiko's Dad came to bring her back home to Japan, and it was a sad departure.

Megan, now that she was 17, wanted to go visit Keiko some time later. I, as a travel agent, was surprisingly asked to make the arrangements for a non-stop flight from JFK to Tokyo for her. (Times do change. I have never traveled alone to another country when I was a kid.) So here's this blond, long haired girl meeting other kids in Japan, who had only seen people with dark hair! Megan slept on a mat on the floor in the basement of their home. The grandparents were in their home also, but the other family members went to work or school. Unfortunately, it was bad timing as Keiko was still in school, and couldn't spend quality time with Megan. They had communicated back and forth prior to the visit, but Megan didn't discern, nor get an understanding, that Keiko would not be able to be with her full time. After a few days, I got the call to bring Megan back home. An expensive misunderstanding!

Communications continued over the years, and when Megan was planning her wedding, she asked Keiko to be her maid-of-honor. The wedding was called off some time later, and Megan has never married, nor has Keiko. Each of them are now in their 40's.

When Sean was older, and began to travel, he went to visit Keiko in Japan. Some communications never die, even long distances.

Interlude...

In November 1999, we were reaching a new millennium, 2000. It was being called Y2K, as researchers were wondering what would happen to the computers when the clock turned at midnight, and we entered 2000. With all their intelligence, it was hard to believe that they couldn't understand it would be a "no-brain-er". Many different theories emerged. As they waited in Australia, it turned out to just be another day.

My father, who was 92 years old in November 1999, was so excited to be a part of another century, and was counting the days until 2000. However, on November 18, he died in his sleep.

In March of the new century, 2000, Paul and I were embarking, with much excitement, on a trip to China. We almost didn't make it.

Going through security at the airport, we headed to our gate. Paul remarked that he was going to the restroom, and I made myself comfortable with my carry-on items surrounding me. Looking around, I realized that I didn't have my handbag. Oh, my God! I left it at security check in. I started running, feeling alarmed that I had lost my handbag with all the pertinent items needed for our trip...airline ticket and passport. There on the gurney, sat my handbag in the corner. No one had taken it. My relief that I could retrieve it was immeasurable. How stupid had I been, as I berated myself! There would have been no trip to China.

Symbol of China

CHAPTER 6

CHINA

China's history is one of the oldest continuous civilizations in the world. The roots of that civilization begin in around 220 BCE, with a prehistoric society. Standardization of script, weights and measures, as well as construction of large infrastructures (including parts of the Great Wall), were landmarks. The golden age of governance , innovation and cultural identity began. Confucianism became the backbone of the state, and the Silk Road opened China to trade with Central Asia and beyond. Marco Polo has been known to begin his travels and reach China, successfully opening up that route. There were many dynasties, and their emperors who led the way as they became a formidable population to be reckoned with.

The People's Republic was founded in 1949, and Mao's rule saw radical campaigns with social and economic consequences. After Mao's death in 1976, many reforms have transformed China into an economic powerhouse. The country has maintained single party rule, while encouraging selective capitalist development, leading to its emergence as a global power.

When we arrived in March 2000 on a tour, we found China to be completely different than we expected. Fashion was in vogue; Mao outfits in their dark drab colors were history. Women paraded in flashy colors with short skirts and high heels, or a more conservative business suit, the same as in Western countries. Men were attired in business suits or mostly sport jackets, vests, white shirt and ties. Even some construction workers were in jackets and ties chipping away at rocks...a funny sight. Plus, men also were in colorful clothes.

The cities were a mix of old buildings, many of which were being torn down to build tall apartment buildings and skyscrapers for offices. Construction cranes were everywhere. Expressways were blossoming in every direction. Their world was going upward and outward, a metamorphosis from another culture. There were some detours here and there to contrast the experience. You couldn't drink the water, and while touring, had to deal with "Eastern bathrooms", which is a hole in the ground. Our guides, who were excellent, had a rating system for use of toilets, from 1 to 5, and if they announced a 1 or 2, I didn't even want to get off the bus.

We started in Shanghai, the largest city in China. Unfortunately, we only had time for a ½ day tour, and it was raining. Actually throughout the trip, for March, it was quite cold. Didn't see much in Shanghai, but it looked promising. We flew out after the tour to Wuhan to pickup the Yangtze River cruise. My next surprise was the ship, Victoria, which had been described as the best Deluxe ship on the river. It was definitely not Deluxe by Western standards. 3 decks and not very big, but pleasant surroundings. It was a ship getting from point A to B, but not a cruise ship. I wondered what the other ships, Regal and President, were like if Victoria was the best. The accommodations were comfortable and the staff very anxious to please. In fact, throughout China, we found all we came in contact with, very friendly and happy to see us.

The Yangtze River was an interesting experience, though not exactly the highlight of the trip. Part of the reason might be that the weather didn't cooperate; it was misty and otherwise cloudy, and might have been more scenic if the sun brightened the scene. There were villages and towns along the river and I expected to see more living, people wise, along the river, but they were in hiding. The river reminded me of the Mississippi, muddy. Sailing through the gorges was nice but supposedly I missed the best part, because I was sick with a stomach issue, and missed the excursion to the "lesser gorges". I heard mixed opinions from the others. Some loved the exhilaration of the "white water" traveling on the "sampans" through the narrow gorges. It was cold and some people got wet. They toured a small village and mixed with the residents. Some opposing viewpoints were, they could skip the whole excursion. Others were lukewarm in their opinions. I was sorry I missed it. On the other hand, as we stayed on the ship, I went to a Chinese doctor who gave me a remedy to settle my stomach. Paul decided to take care of our laundry. The doctor was cheaper than what he paid to have the laundry done.

On the ship one evening, they were teaching us the game of Mah Jongg. It's very prevalent in China as a game played by men. As we drove through towns, we saw men playing the board game outside buildings. It actually started in China, before coming to California at the beginning of the 20th century. I've been playing the game since I was a teenager. As I watched my mother play with her friends, she taught me the game, and I've been playing it since then. In America, it appears to be played by women, and in The Villages where I live, it's hugely popular.

The biggest event on the river was to be the biggest Dam in the world, being built stemming the flow of the river and displacing whole communities that lived alongside. Called the Three Gorges Dam, construction began in 1994.

The largest lake will form and as the waters rise along the river behind it, it will flood the area up to 540 feet. By the year 2009, the whole area we toured with its villages and towns will be underwater, gone forever. The dam is being built to control flooding and give China hydro-electric power. It did become fully operational in 2012 when the final generator was installed, and did become the largest hydro-electric power in the world.

We left the Yangtze River at Chongquing, a mountain city, and then traveled 3 hours to Dazu, where there's famous religious statues enshrined in a cave setting... interesting. We stayed overnight in a 3 star hotel, and the beds were like sleeping on concrete. The trip back to Chongquing was only a plus because the farmlands are the most beautiful I ever saw. Whether terraced or flat, they were laid out like a patchwork quilt, sectioned in squares, triangles and circles, each patch a different color or design, growing vegetables. No fields of one crop here. The commune system is also mostly history, with farmers being allowed to rent land, and sell their own products through a free market or sell back to the government. Restrictions are still one child for one family, except for farmers, who if the first child is a girl, are allowed to try for a second, hoping for a boy to help them till the land. But that was the limit at that time to control the size of the population. For one period of time, they were allowing girls to be adopted, until it became apparent that you need females to produce children.

Tulips originated in China. We think of Holland as famous for tulips and I visited there in 2024. The huge variety and colors were beautiful in both places.

We flew to Xian, a delightful city mixed with the old look of China and the new look of "emerging China". Construction was everywhere. We wandered the streets and mixed with the local residents, even venturing into modern department stores. Very upbeat lifestyles, yet watched them partake of their meals in the outside food stalls, which is still the custom. Of course, McDonald's, Domino's Pizza and KFC were in each of the cities we visited.

Terracotta Warriors

The trip to see the Terracotta Warriors was a highlight. Built 2000 years ago, they were mostly broken by an invading army. This was discovered when they were unearthed in the 1970's. Along with approximately 8000 warriors in amazing detail, are horses and chariots, which were to complement the army and protect the first emperor after he died and entered the next world. The pottery figures and horses were baked in a kiln and later were all colorfully painted. The warriors had different faces and expressions, with real bronze weapons and wooden chariots. We could see some of the figures headless and broken apart.

It is all being restored and was fascinating to see. UNESCO has inscribed the site on the World Heritage list. It is not only pride for the Chinese, but also part of the cultural wealth in the world. Before we came, we had heard about its significance, even though we hadn't known the figures were broken. I'm glad we got to see it.

Beijing was our next stop and as we left the airport and drove into the city, it could have been any major city in the United States, together with construction cranes everywhere. All this emergence is only since the beginning of the 90's. In 1991, there were 2 hotels for tourists, and in 2000, there are over 70. The expressways and roads had more cars than anywhere else we had seen. In contrast, it goes by ability to pay. In Shanghai, registering the car costs as much as buying the car, whereas in Beijing, the registration is only a small fee. Yet the contrast of bicycle traffic was still apparent. There were an enormous amount of bicycle traffic merging with the cars and buses, which though they have their own lanes on the straightaway, at the intersections which don't always have traffic lights, it's quite a sight. You could sit and watch from an upper view and it would be a days entertainment.

I must call your attention to the fact that my observations noted herewith were made when we visited 25 years ago in 2000. Now in 2025, China has grown well beyond its original transformation.

However, our visit to the Great Wall doesn't change as the years pass by. It actually made the trip worthwhile. We were in awe of this feat which definitely belongs as one of the 8 Wonders of the World. Thousands of years ago, they began building this over mountains for a distance of 3000 miles, and it boggles your mind as to how they did it. It was an endurance test to climb this very steep area for about a ½ mile up the mountain to a covered break point, walking on irregular steps. It was even more enduring trying to come back down. It was so steep, you had to hold yourself at a slant backward, and at some points where it turned, I just sat down and my butt took it one step at a time.

The Forbidden City is massive, about a ½ mile long and 1/3 mile wide. The Emperors lived in many, many elaborate buildings on the property. Quite a beautiful site!

My husband shared an office with a Chinese man, who lived in the United States for many years. However, when he began contemplating marriage, he contacted his family in China to find him a bride. When the task was completed, he married the woman, and remained in America. It was more important for him to maintain his culture, and live with the right spouse, who would provide the proper home for him.

I can say that Beijing, and what we experienced there, was the highlight of the whole trip, and when we left, it was with fond memories.

Chapter 7

Malaysia

As a travel agent, I won a trip to Malaysia. It was very exciting to be embarking with anticipation, to another part of Asia that I was completely unfamiliar with. The offer was to stay at a beach resort, but as I was a Floridian, accustomed to beaches, I wanted to be in the heart of Malaysia. Hotels were then arranged for us in different regions.

Malaysia, which occupies parts of Borneo, goes back thousands of years to pre-historic times. Though it was ruled and influenced by many countries, including the British, it is now an independent country. It emerged from Sultans to Prime Ministers. Some of its religious factions have been Hindu and Buddhist, but Islam has made an impact, and now the primary religion. It descends from the 15th century kingdom that spread Islam in Southeast Asia, and shaped political and cultural identity. Serving as a moderate Muslim majority, Malaysia often acts as a bridge between the Islamic world and the West.

Old and new architecture

Flying from Tampa, we arrived in Kuala Lumpur, the capital. We didn't need to reset our watches because it was a 12 hour differential, based on the local time, and a day earlier. Ascertaining that it was going to be special holiday celebration, we looked forward to the festivities. However, after we checked into our hotel, we laid down on the bed to relax, fell asleep, and missed all the action.

When we set out the next day to explore our surroundings, we discovered a city of contrasts, a convergence of the old and the new. There were multiple skyscrapers mixed with beautiful architecture depicting an older era. The buildings had character in shades of gold, with circular roofs in what appeared to be red glass. To me, it was a site that stimulated my senses. How I wish other cities around the world, as they modernize, held on to the relics of the past.

As we strolled around the city, we saw a diversity of culture. We came upon a sport that we were told was a popular cultural activity. It entailed a competition of tossing a top onto a platform.

Top spinning

The tops are wound so tightly that they can spin for about an hour. After the participant circles his body round and round to build up strength, he tosses the top towards its goal. After it lands, and is carried off, a little oil is added for lubrication to help it keep spinning. We watched in fascination.

Another area had a group playing jazz. We enjoyed the music and watching people dancing around. It looked like we could have been in any other Western nation.

The whole area was filled with many people, and what appeared to be tourists, or maybe residents, but all having a good time. You could hear the sounds of many languages all taking pleasure in the scene.

Going into a food market, however, as we went into the produce section, there were many selections of fruits and vegetables we never saw before. When we went into the restaurants, we tried some of those on the menu that we were unfamiliar with, but tasted good. The Malaysians were friendly and accommodating, making us feel very welcome.

We were staying in Malaysia over a week, and so we had the time to explore other parts of the country. We took local transportation to bring us to an area we were told had a Mosque whose unique architecture we should see. After settling into a local hotel, we hired a guide. He took us to the Mosque. It was off the beaten path, and something to write home about. We were quite impressed with its unusual shape, and made out of steel, glass and crystal. As a woman, I wasn't allowed inside, but Paul said it was quite spacious and colorful.

Our guide also brought us to see huge turtles, over 100 years old, in retirement in a large compound. These sites, I'm sure are quite normal to local residents, but to us, it was unique.

In the hotel, after dinner, we ventured into the bar, where there was a 3 piece band, playing what seemed to be Western music. They sent around paper to the small assembled group, and asked for any requests. The first request that they played was “Hava Nigilah”, which is a Hebrew folk song. Paul and I couldn't believe we were sitting in Malaysia listening to that song.

Malaysia is special because it embodies the complex, layered story of Southeast Asia: ancient trade, colonial history, ethnic pluralism, religious diversity and rapid modern transformation, all set against a backdrop of ecological richness. We noticed much of it, as we witnessed lush landscapes on our way to Penang, a Malaysian island, and our next stop.

Arriving at our hotel, and entering our room, I noticed an arrow on the ceiling. When I inquired about its significance, I was told it pointed to Mecca for Muslim prayers. Interesting to relate it to Judaism, where sanctuaries in Synagogues are in the direction of Jerusalem. Christians? Not aware of any pertinence with Christians or other religions.

Penang's heritage streets, especially in Georgetown, it's capital, are a vibrant tapestry of history, architecture and multicultural life. It's been a World Heritage site since 2008, and is a living museum into the lives of people, food and stories. The narrow streets are a mix of shophouses, mosques, temples, churches and clan houses. Shophouses are the backbone of Penang's streetscape... deep buildings serve as shops and residences in several styles. Each shophouse tells a story, not just of wealth or utility, but of cultural blending; Chinese guilds, Indian Muslim traders, and Eurasian families.

On occasions, you can see chariots and processions. Taoist rites may be seen moving along the lanes with live music, paper effigies and incense. There might be Chinese funeral processions, or Chinese New Year lion dances.

Blending the old and new, plus protecting heritage while accommodating modern life, characters of every kind, past and present, still wander about.

There was more to see. A tram ferries visitors to Penang Hill, featuring dramatic views, shops and restaurants. You can go to North Borneo, where there are a biodiversity of orangutans, rhinoceroses and tapirs, which are hoofed mammals related to horses.

We strolled in Penang and went to a snake temple. Venomous snakes are in abundance, but are not aggressive, due to a form of incense in the air. There were all types and colors of the snakes, but you wouldn't want to touch any while they were in their stupor. We went into a cave, which had many cave paintings related to many scenes of animals and people.

We ate in a restaurant, where I had the best tomato soup I had ever had. I asked the waiter if the chef would give me the recipe, and he came back to tell me the chef would comply. When we received our bill, there was the recipe: tomatoes, carrots and onions, no amounts. I thanked the chef, knowing I could never make it on my own.

Looking back on our visit to Malaysia, I was the most enthusiastic, and believed it to be one of the best countries to experience.

CHAPTER 8

INDONESIA

Departing from Singapore, we were on a Holland America cruise, traversing Indonesia and ending in Sydney, Australia. It is now 2002. Our first port of call was to be Jakarta, but there were protests disrupting the government, and we couldn't land. For us, a window opened up, and instead of one day, when we would be in Bali, it was now going to be 2 days. That surely makes us happy.

Indonesia is a huge country with over 17,000 islands, spread across 3400 miles along the equator, between the Indian and Pacific oceans.

Previously controlled by other nations over the centuries, like the Dutch, it gained its independence after World War II. It operates as a Presidential Republic, with Jakarta as its capital, but with continuing conflicts and natural disasters over the years. Indonesia sits along the "ring of fire", so it's prone to volcanoes and earthquakes.

Despite its large population and densely populated regions, Indonesia has vast areas of wilderness that support one of the highest levels of diversity. There's an abundance of towering mountains, extreme river systems, vast lakes and coral reefs. Notable is that it's a valuable region for trade, because it has lots to offer.

As the ship continued along its path, we stopped at the island of Semaring. On the tour, we came upon a site where an ancient temple was unearthed. The populace thought it was a mountain. What a revelation! I recall that in other countries I've visited, archaeologists made discoveries of cities buried for centuries. Archaeology is fascinating, as there are many opportunities for wonderment and surprises.

The highlight of the cruise, Bali! We were so excited to reach it. There is something so magical about Bali, that it stirs a desire in your dreams to someday be in that locale.

According to BBC Travel that I read about, Bali is one of the world's best islands, ranking 2nd after Santorini, Greece. The entertainer, David Bowie, wanted his ashes to be scattered in Bali. That is how it is revered.

Muslims are the most popular group throughout the nation, with almost 90% participation. However, in Bali, Hindu is the dominate religion, and unlike any other. Daily life revolves around rituals, offerings and ceremonies that blend Hindu beliefs and ancestor worship. Bali is often called the "island of the Gods", not only for its stunning natural beauty, but also its deeply, spiritual and artistic culture.

There's a concept that teaches a balance between humans and the divine; humans and nature; humans and one another. This belief governs everything from architecture to agriculture, creating an atmosphere where visitors sense a deep harmony in the environment.

The festivals include moon celebrations. As for the cremation ceremonies, the dead are sent off with music, dance and fire. A commentary that I've heard, makes you think it's worthy and highly regarded. When we are born, there is nothing known about that person yet. But when we die, we've filled our lives with qualities in relationships and accomplishments. So it should be celebrated.

Small palm leaf baskets filled with flowers, rice and incense are placed several times a day on shrines, sidewalks and even car dashboards. These acts are not just religious, but expressions of gratitude and harmony with nature and spirit.

Beautiful architecture are in Temples. Every family has a personal temple of all sizes in their own backyards.

As we strolled around, we saw statues everywhere. They were draped in colorful cloth. When we inquired, we were told the different colors reflect religious meaning. We could feel the spirituality in the air, as we met the Balinese.

Statues covered in cloth

Art is everywhere. It isn't confined to museums. Dance, music, woodworking, sculptures and painting are a living, breathing part of everyday life.

At a booth, we were impressed with the woodworking. Right in front of us was a creation of the heads of 2 women adjacent to each other, with crowns of temples on top. It was so finely detailed, that we bought it to be placed in our curio cabinet.

We watched the Balinese dance dramas. They are renowned for their highly developed Barong dances that are traditional and mesmerizing. The Barong dance is one of the island's most iconic and deeply symbolic cultural performances. It is more than a dance, but a dramatic representation of the eternal battle between good and evil, rooted in traditions and mythology. The percussion music and performing arts add to the mix.

Shadow puppetry is performed depicting Hindu epics. The Indonesian Film Festival is held yearly, and welcomed locally.

We took a tram up a mountain, and saw the rice terraces that seemed artistically designed in patterns. They were colorful and geometrically shaped. The rice farming follows traditional irrigation systems, which are based on cooperation and temple rituals.

Rich coral reefs host a wide range of marine life, like giant sunfish and manta rays, as well as moray eels.

Our visit was magical, beautiful and a wonderful sense of peace. A portrait to remember.

Chapter 9

Asian/American Club

Following my interest in the Asian culture, I belong to an Asian/American Club in my community. China, Thailand, Korea, Japan, India and Vietnam are the countries that are represented in the club. We have individuals who spent a major part of their lives living in these countries, and are pleased to share their culture in entertainment and food with us. Each month, another country is highlighted by providing us with dinner and performances from their country. I find the meals are similar in their content and taste. However, when it's India's turn, I have no taste for the spices in their food, and refrain from coming to their event.

But otherwise, I witness dancing and musical instruments being played. The percussion is very intriguing, and very different from Western instruments. The drums are very large and the sound that is emitted from them is unusual to our ears. We're watching them pound on multiple drums with their batons. They cross over hitting on adjacent drums in alternate directions in perfect sync with each other. The string instruments are also different from our Western ones, creating music in different tones.

The dancing routines are graceful and enjoyable to watch. The dancers are dressed in their Asian outfits, and seem to be concentrating on the country they left behind. Each performance is an insight into a world half way across the world.

A special event once a year is the Chinese New Year approximately held in January. The "dragon" dancers circle the room in between the tables. The singing and accompanying music fill the air, and the food served is a specialty. I never want to miss it, and make sure to secure my reservation.

Participation in this Asian/American Club is about 50% Asian and 50% Caucasian. There are many mixed marriages between the two, and it appears the Caucasian men are connected to the Asian women. The men seem to be much older, and many of the woman younger. But the attraction to each other might have stemmed from when the men were in combat in the Asian countries.

Belonging to his club has rounded out the good feelings I have for Asian culture.

Epilogue

Walking Through Asia kept us on our toes. As we adapted to the time zones, we branched out to ascertain the wonders of a new culture; a new world. There were multi-ethnic individual histories. We recognized how they kept distinct identities, and moved forward parallel to each other. Our feet never left the ground, but skipped along with excitement like a child learning something new each day.

As the years go by, I have many memories of adventures that are indelible in my mind... the photos, the souvenirs that embrace me. When we look back on our lives, we always have stories to tell to our contemporaries and to our children, who they themselves have so much to look forward to. For us, enjoy the sunshine around you.

ABOUT THE AUTHOR

As I continue to write, I find subjects that intrigue my mind, and want to be put on paper. Each book is very different from the others, but readers have told me that it fascinates them and enjoy reading them.

Made in the USA
Coppell, TX
02 January 2026

67665195R00056